JULIE McNEILL is the Poet-[...] Club Charitable Trust, the [...] established – attached to [...] UK, perhaps in the world. [...] Collection, set up to preserve and protect Scotland's footballing heritage.

Julie's work has been recently commissioned by BBC Sport Scotland and the Scottish Poetry Library and in 2024 she won The Burrell Collection Hidden Gems poetry competition.

Recent poetry collections include *Something Small* (Drunk Muse Press 2023) and *Ragged Rainbows* (HybridDreich 2021) and the award winning non-fiction book for children *Mission Dyslexia* (JKP Books 2021). She spends much of her time working with neurodivergent children and adults.

CAMPBELL RAMAGE is a photographer and picture editor based in the West End of Glasgow. A long-suffering Partick Thistle fan, he can often be found standing in a state of zen-like calm as his team battle it out at the Palace of the Gallus.

Away from football, Campbell enjoys wandering the streets of his home city in search of images that capture his eye, and his imagination.

A recurring theme of Campbell's work is 'Positivity'. His 2022 portrait exhibition *Maryhill is Wonderful* won Scottish Parliamentary approval as he sought to highlight the people who make a positive contribution to everyday life in the area.

We Are Scottish Football

Poems by
JULIE McNEILL

Photography by
CAMPBELL RAMAGE

Luath Press Limited
EDINBURGH
www.luath.co.uk

First published 2024

ISBN: 978-1-80425-157-7

The author's right to be identified as author of this book
under the Copyright, Designs and Patents Act 1988
has been asserted.

The paper used in this book is recyclable. It is made from
low-chlorine pulps produced in a low-energy,
low-emission manner from renewable forests.

Printed and bound by
Robertson Printers, Forfar

Typeset in 11 point Sabon by
Main Point Books, Edinburgh

For Glasgow, my first love.
Julie McNeill

For Sineádin, Rosie and Ru – my favourite team.
Campbell Ramage

Contents

PART TWO: For the Love of the Game

Introduction

2024 IS THE road to the Euros, there's a great buzz in the air of anticipation and possibility. I'm obsessed with the weird and wonderful routes, ruses and remarkable geographical idiosyncrasies that will enable the Tartan Army and all who follow them to converge in Munich this summer to watch Scotland play Germany in the opening game.

Though my poet's bag is packed and I wouldn't miss it for the world, my own love of football began long before the Euros.

When I moved to Glasgow 30 years ago I had no idea of the footballing secrets that lay overgrown and undiscovered across the city. Little by little they were introduced to me – could that quiet wee bowling club in the Southside be the first purpose-built, enclosed football ground? Was the first floodlight a searchlight? How many Hampden Parks are there? Women were… banned? What's cricket got to do with the formation of the SFA? Did a Scottish man really get the ball rolling in Argentina?

The more I found out the more I wanted to know.

I was very lucky in 2020 to meet through the Hampden Collection a group of volunteers who were making this their mission: to preserve and protect Scotland's footballing heritage. They had recently discovered a map of the first Hampden Park, I was writing poetry for the Scottish Women's National Team as it swept the nation to the World Cup in France, my daughter was watching on wide-eyed, and there was so much to be proud of.

People think football and poetry unlikely bedfellows but I can't think of anything that drives passion, despair, disappointment, elation and pride like football. The people's game, what's more poetic than that? I'm fascinated by the rituals, the traditions, the stories and the connections made possible through following club or country. I think, despite its many downfalls, football is a force for good in the world.

In Scotland we should be incredibly proud of our footballing legacy – off the pitch as much as on it, we were the trailblazers. The modern passing and running game of football would not be what it is today without the pioneering 'Scotch Professors', who transformed the way football was played in the late 1870s – as a team game.

Of course the history of Scottish football extends far beyond the 21 sites of Football's Square Mile in Glasgow. Go out and uncover those gems in your own communities, hear the stories of your clubs and preserve and protect them with everything you have.

When I started writing this collection I approached Campbell Ramage, a brilliant photographer I have known since my early days in Glasgow. Campbell tackled the project with creativity, understanding and a generosity of spirit. I'm forever grateful to him for jumping in with two feet and bringing so much to the table.

This collection is about Passion, Poetry and Preservation.

WE are Scottish Football.

Julie McNeill
April 2024

PART ONE

Football's Square Mile

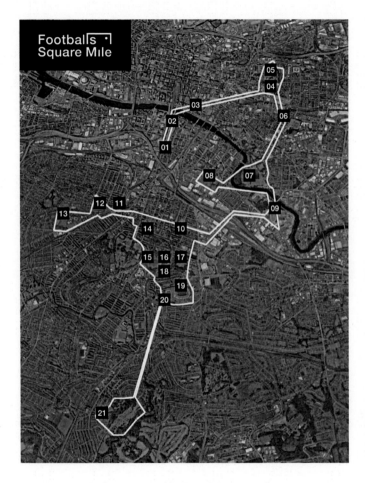

Map reproduced by permission of The Football's Square Mile Company Limited.

Key to Sites

29 Eglinton Street, the birthplace of Alexander Watson Hutton, dubbed the father of Argentinian football.

Rollin

A laddie fae the Gorbals
orphant bi five
but aa scholar,
bore lang an sair
at the wurld an its airts,
an cam tae the thocht
hinmaist at the wey tae chynge
things fer the guid
was Fitba.

There are veesionaries
an veesionaries,
ilka mon's ingine
ne'er truly foon oot
intil efter he dees.

When Watson Hutton
went tae the
Scots School in Buenos Aires
he stairtit sumhin.

Mebbe it was his bousy tache
or his native gallusness,
bit mair lik his virr

that gart five hunnert weans,
an efter that thir pals,
tae pass an rin
lik Scotch Professors.

Fer ilka action there is an
equal an conter reaction.
He stairtit the ba rollin.

Roots and Wings

All we can do
for our children is to
provide roots and wings:
a place they've come from,
a fence line and a full blue sky
to explore raggedly, or joyfully,
like a skein of geese.

Fresh from West,
we were International.
Itching to start something
at Bridge Street
in person or by letter
they drew a boundary line
by association.

You might think that
a small act:
Queen's Park and
seven cricket clubs
seeing enough of this sport
to help others play, form
and join together

but yesterday I watched
Buckie Thistle battle
the tornado of Celtic,
Spartans take a goal
off Hearts and Forfar
go toe-to-toe with Hibs.
Dreams are nurtured in such ways.

The Tifo glowed with
Here for the Good
a storm ripped on and
the tidal force of football
swept across Scotland as fierce
and strong as those
first momentous days

but here we nod to the
the risk takers and cricketers
who ventured into that big blue sky
to play fitba in the winter
then back to the warmth of the crease
when the sun shone.

Bridge Street, the birthplace of the Scottish Football Association.

Havelock Buildings, East Howard Street, the birthplace of Third Lanark.

Hi-Hi

Scarlet strips
worn like war paint
to repel
the Rangers,
Queen's Park,
Napoleon Bonaparte.

No matter who
attacked
they held
that tight
defensive line
around Mount Florida,

but defeat
was an inside job:
in an ageless story
of courage
against penny pinching,

art against avarice
the club was
choked out
by greed.

Amen

That red T could be
the Tartan Army flag
whole regiments
fuelled by the froth of it.

Forget your Golden Arches
and Harris Tweed
or lines of See You Jimmys
this brewery sits on druid land,

even its name
means the priest's path.
I get off the train
where we've been packed

and stacked like sardines,
my face pressed into an armpit,
the pheasant feather
of a Glengarry stuck

in the heaving doors,
and wade through
the crush and pish
to the bar, the altar,

and that first gulp
of cool council lager
is better than communion wine,
it's the most sacred of blessings.

Drygate, where Tennent's Caledonian Breweries began.

Glasgow Necropolis, William Dick SFA secretary 1875–80
is buried here.

City of the Dead

*Glasgow is a bit like Nashville, it doesn't care much
for the living but it really looks after the dead.*
—Billy Connolly

Cross the Bridge of Sighs
navigate the topography:
the winding paths meandering
skywards above the city's

spans and muscles. Search him out
carrying the emblems
of Rosebery's past,
the primrose and pink flowers.

Stroke the cool stone chiselled
into a football, remember
the greatest victory over England,
the guts and skill of Andrew Watson.

Think of the rule book placed in the hands
of the Marquis of Lorne. Stand back
to the view of Glasgow,
stretched out like a friend, a lover,

and the great river bleeding to the sea,
to Ireland, England, Canada.
Then listen carefully to the whispers.
The dead can travel, as you know.

For Good

On Abercromby Street
The Calton, Glasgow's
East End

Brother Walfrid
rejoiced as the young Hibbies
of Edinburgh

brought the Scottish cup home.
He thought *whit if our lads
had the same?*

A *bright new fitba team
wedded from the start
to the common weal:*

*a hot meal apiece
filling the bellies o the weans
in the East End.*

It's the poor look after the poor
in Scotland, always was, and is.
Scottish football is twinned

with good causes from
the Gorbals to Gaza:
The people's game

for the people's good,
let's ne'er foryet it.

St Mary's Church, Brother Walfrid dreams up Celtic Football Club.

Flesher's Haugh, the site of Rangers Football Club's first game.

Four Lads Had a Dream

When young Moses
walked across
a west end park
with the two Peters
and that lad William,

they mustn't have
looked much. Just
laddies they were
around sixteen with
a mad teenage dream

to start a football team.
That bit the Gareloch
rowers held their kickabout
fresh from the river
was as good a place as any,

the flat land
that held the pavilion
of the Bonnie Prince
when he demanded
the city provide

thousands of
bonnets and boots
to fit out his Highland troops,
that stretch
of butcher's land,

and young Moses
cutting straight
across it like a cleaver,
marking one half
of that grass green

one forever blue.

Archie's Watch

Archie, can you see us now
far from our white bowler hats?
Do you chart how far we've travelled,
the legacy you've left?

These clubs are more than badges
more than fixtures, leagues and scores,
there's something else that happens
when you step inside those doors.

Folk do their growing-up there
a place to safely make mistakes,
somewhere to let their hair down
a gathering of mates.

But some who come along
flip conventions on their head,
they bring with them an energy,
a fire to do something else instead.

I wonder how you capture
what it means for folk to fit,
to find a sort of family,
support, encouragement and kin.

It's a safe harbour in the dark days
when you can't shut out the dread
cross those white lines of safety, take the
weight off your weary head.

You started Clydesdale Cricket Club
you led the SFA,
threw money in for the Scottish Cup,
made it possible for folk to play.

Archie thank you for the vision,
the energy you've shown,
for leaving us a legacy
we're proud to call our own.

Southern Necropolis, resting place of Archibald Campbell, first president of the Scottish Football Association and founder of Clydesdale Cricket Club.

Who Dares?

I'd have given anything to see them
become champions of the world,
Sadie and the ladies
dodging, feinting, swerving
round the Dick Kerr Girls.

They showed them how it's done,
shimmying past the cross, bald men
who declared it was wrong
for anyone to dare
to look at women footballers.

They kept the head
and stood up tall
when bans, fans, associations
told them to stick
to *folk football:*

you know, the games
where men
chaperone, tie their hands
behind their backs
let the ladies score,

then having chivalrously lost,
take back the ball. This stadium
saw the beginning
of the end to that.
These girls were women
worth watching.

In 1923 Rutherglen Ladies Football Club became 'world champions' at
Shawfield after they defeated the famous Dick, Kerr Ladies of Preston.

Football Under Electric Light
Old Cathkin, Govanhill, 1878 –
first floodlight use in Scotland

It was less floodlight
more searchlight:
a fifty foot tower
and a single beam

following the ball.
Players left stumbling
in darkness or suddenly
blinded, the lamp

too fast, too slow,
off the pace.

My son plays every evening
in the glow of the security light:
the grass is a muddy bog,
posts lean to the left

and the scarecrow goalie
has lost a gloved hand.
The light shines too bright

'Old' Cathkin Park in Govanhill became the home of Third Lanark
Football Club. In 1878, this was where floodlights were used
for the first time.

then off, then bright again.
I see his beautiful face,
strobed and weather-beaten
determined to play the game.
It doesn't occur to me

to tell him to wait
for the daylight to come back.

Follow the Spiders

The cobweb in the graveyard
is starting to fray,
its intricate patterns
ripped by the wind.

It is ragged and misshapen
and yet I cannot
take my eyes off it,
every gossamer strand

3 Eglinton Terrace, the birthplace of 'The Spiders', Queen's Park
Football Club.

joined and positioned
with care, the rings
spreading out
like ripples of water,

knowledge and instinct
combining to create
such skill and art.
Follow the spiders,

they say, they will show you
the way to the source,
to where the magic
of the pass and run began.

Let's Get Physical

They met here to throw hammers,
toss cabers, vault poles, build muscle
and feel the stretch and sinew
of their bodies grow.

There were no fancy monitors,
no induction or goal setting,
no app to perfect their stance
or hands-free for the iPhone,

and not a single man counted
their steps between here and home.
They could feel the good, though,
in their lungs and arms,

in their hearts and heads.
I see the early morning mums'
group lift their growing toddlers
high overhead in my local park,

they push buggies back and forth
over the bridge, jog at varying speeds
up the hill. They smile and coo
at their babies and relish time outside

their homes. They celebrate their strength,
their health. In lockdown the canal path
was a steady stream of joggers, a log jam
of family bike rides, a glut of hoverboarding teens.

When we strip it back, as we are sometimes
required to do, the body knows
what it needs. Glasgow will always lend you
a corner, a park, a path.

Just bring your own guts and determination.

Near Lorne Terrace, Pollokshields, the founding members of Queen's Park Football Club first practised hammer throwing, putting, tossing the caber, pole vaulting and other exercises. In 2023 Glasgow received recognition for its sporting legacy and was awarded the title 'European Capital of Sport'.

Dubbed 'The Forgotten Hampden' and temporary home of Queen's Park Football Club, Titwood is the home to Clydesdale Cricket Club established in 1848. 'The Dale' was commissioned for their 175th birthday in 2023.

The Dale

*On the beautiful meadow, surrounded by stately
trees and green hedges, away from the din of
hammers and free from the pall of city smoke a large
assemblance of ladies and gentlemen watched the
animated and truly scientific game and appeared to
be much interested in the issue.*
—Archibald Campbell, founder, 1848

In their first game against Greenock
they wore white bowler hats
with streaming green and yellow ribbons
they were quickly on the attack,

many seeds are grown
and more are nurtured here,
175 years of cricket,
a reason for us all to cheer.

In the winter they played football
and a 'fledgling' Rangers side
were honoured to play against them,
they were flying high.

Twenty-two hockey GB caps,
they invented Law Fifteen,
fourteen ladies' titles in a row,
and the finest welcome that was ever seen.

Seven football internationalists,
six for rugby too,
one Scottish Cup final-
ok they lost 0-2

but against the mighty Queen's Park,
pioneers of the game.
Clydesdale more than played its
part when its members set up the SFA.

Not content to leave it there
they won the first rugby cup,
is there any sport they cannot do?
They win with stick, or foot or bat

Hockey, tennis and the Harriers
keep the club ahead of the race
as recognition grows
for the proud history of this place.

Olympians, athletes,
the best club around

and do you know the Scottish Cup
is made of five Clydesdale pounds?

A place where everyone is welcome,
all voices heard
cricket's gift to Glasgow,
to Scotland and the world.

The Women Before Her

Not yet six
she half sits,
half stands,

her body fizzing,
fixated on the pink
shirts before her.

She's singing for
Shelley's army and
doesn't miss a beat,

eighteen thousand
voices, for our
girls, for our game,

for her Scotland.
They show us
what women

can do when
we raise each other.
She believes in

The Rose Reilly Pub is named after the only Scottish player to win the World Cup. Rose started her career for Stewarton Boys with the help of a short haircut to disguise the fact that she was a girl. She went on to play in France and Italy, winning the French and Italian leagues in the same season, and won the Women's World Cup for Italy in 1984.

the women who
save it themselves,
the girls standing

ready to gie it laldy
and the ones who
laid the ground,

before her,
shoulder to shoulder,
lighting the way.

Kickabout

These games are won
and lost in moments,
in scuffs and snatches,
trips and pullbacks.

Plant your feet then,
raise your heads
and see what you have achieved,
games lost, games won.

Our expectations grow
because you made it so.
Tonight, my daughter watched
you play – she dreams

of being you, one day.
Her jacket's in the wash again,
it's been masquerading
as a goalpost in the mud.

She's ditched the school skirt
for a football strip.
She doesn't measure
her game in inches,

the mud-splats and missed shots
bring her back to the centre spot
where she will rise and fall
and rise again.

Queen's Park Recreation Ground. In 1867 a group of men spotted
members of the Young Men's Christian Association playing football
here and joined in. They subsequently went on to form
Queen's Park Football Club.

Echoes

On the discovery of the First Hampden map

On Glasgow's Southside
by a rose-scented garden,
a man waits patiently
for the post.

Too afraid of the echoes
he walks from Cathkin Park,
to the cricket ground, to Hampden and back,
to the old bowling club,
to the pavilion, to the beginning.

It's in his hands, now
and so with trepidation
he tears the envelope open
and scans the railway map inside,

fragments of legends gather
from across the decades,
the way shards of iron
bend towards a magnetic force.

They form the words that change everything –
'*football ground*' he smiles,
right here by the railway line
as sure now as the earth beneath our feet.

Hampden Bowling Club is the site of the first Hampden Park.
The first two Scottish Cup finals were hosted here. It is the world's
first purpose-built, enclosed international football ground. The map
proving the exact location of the site was located in March 2017.

The Ghost Stadium

It's a secret garden,
no need for a magic key
but you'd walk right past it
if you didn't know.

Creep up the tree-lined path
and feel the branches
fold over you,
covering the exits. All ways

back to the rush of the road
you were standing on
just seconds ago are
now obscured.

Out the corner of your eye
you will glimpse an opening,
an expanse of green,
grey terraces mud-slicked

and mossed, reclaimed
by land and time. It's dog walkers'
ground now, office workers'
lunchtime escape

The second Hampden Park. Cathkin Park, Glasgow's 'ghost stadium' hosted the first 'Championship of the World' in 1888 where Scottish Cup holders Renton beat FA Cup holders West Bromwich Albion 4–1.

a thinking space. Mulched
and rusted like a memorial
to a child who died too young.
Nobody wants to shift a blade

of grass in case the memories
vaporise. I think of it as a doorway:
I lean on the red rust and feel
I've discovered the *Mary Celeste*.
An unsinkable place.

Hampden Terrace, named after the parliamentarian and 'people's hero' John Hampden who became famous for standing up to King Charles I and refusing to pay taxes levied by the Monarch (dubbed the 'ship money') on the people without parliament's consent.

Revolution

I like to think he placed
a gentle hand on their backs,
encouraged them to be brave.
Builders George and Alexander Eadie

picked a person of principle
to give name to their toil, their street.
When *The Spiders* rented a corner
of Queen's Park, John Hampden's name

loomed over their shoulder
from the terrace. A revolutionary,
a hero, someone who stood up
to the King, refused to pay his 'Ship Money'

and risked a charge of treason.
His defiant voice lives on, I hear it
in the beat of the Hampden drum
and in the hearts of the men and women

who brandish the badge, live to play.
I've felt it, when everything is left
on the pitch. Everything is risked
and the Hampden roar is all that's left
to carry us home.

From Hampden Park with Heavy Feet

We had 90 minutes to prove –
we were practically a shoe-in
the flights were booked
for Qatar and Cardiff,
just 90 minutes to do.

The Tifo Saltire glistened proudly –
we were freed from desire-
the blue and white,
the blue and white,
this was going to be our day.

But then came the blue and yellow –
the flag we've all been rooting for –
and despite a rally at the end
we just didn't make the score.

The sun shone down upon their glory
and we tasted the defeat,
dragging bucket hats and scarfs and flags
from Hampden Park with heavy feet.

But today we dust them off again,
today we hope for something more
today we tell ourselves,
we'd rather go to Germany than Qatar.

Hampden Park, Scotland National Team Stadium, home of the Tartan Army
and the famous 'Hampden Roar'.

'Lesser' Hampden, The City Stadium, was opened in 1924 and, amongst other uses, has been requisitioned during World War 2, performed as a warm-up ground for the Commonwealth Games and stood in for the national stadium during periods of refurbishment.

Lesser

There's not much that's lesser
about this Scotland super sub,
waiting in the shadows,

living under a Big Hampden cloud
like a jealous wee sister. You'd
easily miss it while your eyes

were dazzled, but this place holds
its own as Commonwealth
warm-up, staging area,

practice ground, an understudy
for the main event.
A wartime base for the Home Guard

and in peacetime
now home to Queen's Park
the first Scotland, the beginning.

The shop front is important,
it hooks folk, reels them in
but football is a patchwork

of good folk doing small things
without praise every day.
The lesser is the good stuff
of the game, I'd say.

Small Acorns

Mist hung low the night before
the clans gathered in celebration.
A glow from pitch-side flats now spotlights

this ground, long since settled underfoot.
Sure of its place in the history books
as the resting place of Pioneers and
Professors.

Great Grandsons walk their ancestors' steps
and children run excitedly to re-enact
the match that changed everything.

Listen closely to the mist-whispers.
Each one, an acorn, a trusted single seed
to anchor our game.

Branches now strong enough
to hold the disappointments
and the shards of pure, unadulterated joy.

Deep roots sustaining new ways of playing,
doors coaxed opened
for fresh shoots in grassroots

and the boot marks made
by the Scotch Professors
are still running rings around the globe.

Cathcart Cemetery, the final resting place of the 'Scotch Professors',
who took the passing and running game of football to the world.

PART TWO

For the Love of the Game

Are you #ThatGuy?

I've been the only woman
squashed between feather and armpit
on the Mount Florida train
on match day:

You on the right train love?

I've kept my mouth shut
at games not wanting to draw
too much attention
even when I've had plenty to say,
like

Why don't you shut the fuck up?

I've pulled my son
and my daughter's hats down
around their heads to block out
the noise.

She'd get it, she'd definitely get it!

I know the statistics:
the crunch of dejection
stamping up the driveway
the rattle of the key in the door

silence.

My daughter will soon be too old
for me to clap my hands
over her ears, my son
now sits with the Young Team

too cool to wear his hat,
all his senses open
to the world, laughter
is his overcoat now.

I should've called it out
when their wide eyes
looked to me for answers.
This year

it took that politician
over six minutes
to read out the names
of the dead.

Phenomenal

They were munitionettes,
canary girls and footballers
taking the spaces
vacated by lovers,

brothers, fathers.
Commentators said
they played '*with vigour
and remarkable dexterity*',

the same dexterity
that turned skin yellow
or brought them out of life
to fuel a war that wasn't theirs.

They saw wee Josie
chip the whole day shift
and dink the ball
into the waiting mouth

of the goal. Phenomenal
women, strong, sinewy,
pacy. In extraordinary times,
they ran that line together.

Pressure

When he asks if we're feeling the pressure,
the answer is we've felt it all our lives.

Just the right amount to squeeze a pal's hand
        when she is breaking,
to cup a daughter's face and tell her she's more
        than good enough.

The extra hours burning the midnight oil to prov
        you're just as smart as them
and to then get up and burn the oil again.

The pressure in your legs when you drive hard
        towards the goal
determined you will earn your place as the team's
        one and only girl.

The pressure to look, or feel, or be as they'd expe
Nothing more and nothing less.

So when he asks if we're feeling the pressure
of a nation on our backs,
our answer is 'Aye'
but we girls know a thing or two about that.

Cuthbert and McGinn

At six she slurped Soleros
outside the Parc de Princes,
juice dripping stickily down fingers
as her brother climbed, and skipped, and danced.

They both shouted 'Flower of Scotland'
skin-soaked by Parisian rain
and marched with the Tartan Army,
stopping traffic with their cheers and waves.

Sat upon a stranger's shoulders
she watched Erin smash it home,
her tummy leapt in expectation
with every cross and throw.

Her brother's leading us to London
crossing numbers off the chart
practicing his 'John McGinn'
in the rain down Barshaw Park.

He'll be singing in Mount Florida
his heart fluttering on the train.
He'll be eating pie and Bovril
on the way to Wembley.

And they'll be with us on the sofa
wearing Cuthbert and McGinn
draped in hope and expectation
as we batten down and coorie in.

From Parc de Princes to Hampden
you build it, they will come.
One nation, two teams
and a summer full of dreams.

Hope

It's always the hope that kills you
the expectation, the 'what ifs?'
the endless machinations
of margins and statistics
and 'aye but remember whens'.

There's nothing logical
about hope,
this perpetual cycle
of belief and despair
we willingly and eagerly
place ourselves on.

We suspend all rational thought,
indulge in pure fantasy,
raise our team above the prize
and go forward wide-eyed,
full-hearted,
full-bodied,
foolhardy.
forward.
With that damned hope in our hearts, again.

Germany

His dad was born in '74.
As we qualified for Germany
he took his first determined steps
on the march with Ally's army.

When Strachan scores in '86,
he's on his daddy's shoulders,
his 1990 soundtrack
is Pavarotti's *Nessun Dorma*.

On his first day in this bright world,
no Scotland could be seen
dad and him lie on the couch
and adopt some other teams.

The sound of vuvuzelas
are slowly lulling him to sleep.
But this year they'll fly to Germany.
This Scotland, his dad and him.

Lone Monochrome

A Buddie before I was born,
womb-clad in black and white,
bedtime stories of Love Street
and Paisley Patterns spun
into my dreams,
I am in with the bricks.

My name, a foundation stone
etched into a stadium wall
when I was small,
monikers like sentinels
guarding a lone monochrome
in a Glaswegian sea choked
with blue and green.

Running the schoolyard gauntlet
against the tide, the day after
the match before: Scottish Cup.
Quarter finals. Paradise.

Everything was massive
as we walked sun-soaked up the Gallowgate
like a couple of black sheep.

As we passed his statue Dad said
that Jinky was better than Messi
and if we kept it to three down by halftime
we'd be doing well.

And then, everything slowed
as I perched like a bird in the top tier
the ball sailed past the giant's last stand
and the scoreboard flickered from 0 to 1.

Aye, ninety minutes on
they had four to our one. But for forty-five
we stopped the unstoppable force
and believed that anything is possible
if you want it enough.

I walk into school, armour on,
I am where I belong.
Standing strong,
banking these moments
as the sea of black carries
and time rages.

Love Street

It used to be Love Street,
shoulder-carried, all standing
'You'll remember this one son'

and me, thirteen, held above his head
in jubilation. I do remember
when St Mirren won

the sea of black crashed
against a tangerine sun.
His face is fading now

twenty-five years on
and I can't feel his arms
around me. I wish I had a photo,

just one. It used to be Love Street
but now the black streets
pour out of cars and bars

and it's all shiny and new.
Now it's me and you, son,
kissing the brick in his name

before every game.
Rituals born and borrowed
from Love Street.

Pass It On

We are nothing without someone to pass to;
an open foot bent to cushion the ball
or a hand to raise up when we inevitably fall
because everybody falls.

The twelfth man or woman
to heat up the car, to get us there,
no matter how far, to dab the skint knees
or give us a much needed ruffle of the hair,

the power is always in the crowd
willing us on.
In the numbers standing proud.
We are all guardians of our history

and as the magic of our game
sweeps us all away
it's our job to remember the build up.
To remember where it started

Who started it
Where and when

and then

to take it as far as we can
before raising our heads to pass it on,
because we are nothing without someone to pass to.

History

The Scotland first eleven shine
from a poster on her bedroom wall:
Caroline, Martha, Jamie-Lee.

I try to trace the thread
following the line that brought
us to this settled ground,

piecing together scrolling, scrolling
I find snippets in footnotes,
addendums, clues buried

in unrelated places,
obscure articles and
off-the-cuff comments.

Headlines such as '*Are you near
Fir Park tomorrow? Take the wife
with you to see the lady footballers.*'

Threads fray and fuse
before I find the end.
It's like holding mist

in your fingertips
wondering where
did your history go?

Level Playing Field

If it's not the huge green pole
it's the steward's head,
and if not them
the barrier on the goal side,
or the opposition fans'
backs when they jump up

to applaud, or furiously vent
their rage. The only way
to know who has scored
is by lugging in
to the noise from the other end,
or ours. Don't think

of cheering, though,
or placing head
in hands in despair,
instead stare straight ahead,
stay mute
like the *vegetable* some
think you are.

Always
an afterthought. Any reaction
might earn you a bottle
flung furiously
at you, the closest
sitting duck.

For in every respect
you have entered
hell in a handcart,
you've been wheeled
behind enemy lines
and instead of that coat

drawn up against the cold
or your team's jersey
proudly put on,
you might as well have worn
a target
on your back.

Scotland, Our Scotland

It's fair to say we're all feeling the trudge,
no sun-soaked, Saltire-draped adventures
in the offing.

That Erin Cuthbert strike at the Parc de Princes
feels like another time, another life,
our pre-Corona.

Go on! Heat up the pie
get the colours on,
slosh hot liquid in the homemade Bovril

and treat yourself
to 90 minutes of hope.
Goodness knows, we need it.

Here we go! Can you picture it, though?
Silverware glinting
in the early evening sun

Shelley Kerr thanking everyone,
Elmslie, Weir and Arnot, arms aloft
crowds crowing and congratulating

in pre-pandemic full-on hugs
and Scotland, our Scotland, arms locked
raising all of us up.

Secret

The bottom drawer
where I usually hide
the Christmas presents
is keeping a big secret.

It holds:
four hooded tops telling us 'We Can Boogie',
two Euros 'Facts and Flags' activity books,
a stencil for the glitter tattoos,
train tickets and a day off school
and the hopes and dreams of two weans
who don't yet know
they are off to Wembley.

Zero Sum Game

Glasgow transforms,
is a zombie apocalypse
a dystopian wasteland

on these days even
the green grass hisses
at the blueness of the sky.

The distant horizon wears
its red like blood and everyone
retreats, or organises.

The small weans in the nursery
part like oil
and water.

They only use the blue
or the green plastic forks,
metal cars, paints, playdoh.

They drink out of blue water
cups or suck from green
cartons. Blue befriends Blue.

Green embraces itself
in the mirror. When they
go home in green cars

to green houses or on
blue bikes scooping adults
spilling out of blue pubs

they learn the flute or the fiddle,
worship the Tricolour or Union Jack.
March or pull the curtains tight.

Non football fans mark '*Old Firm Day*'
on calendars with a large X
the way doors were branded

to ward off evil spirits.
They hoard their supplies
the day, the week, before

so they don't need to venture
into the streets, cut their path
through the fog of fear and hate.

A people's sport
for the people's good? Four lads
had a dream? Let it be

a nil-nil draw, everyone stay safely
in their corners
for this zero sum game.

Set the Stage

She dusts the dugout
and sharpens the sunlight,
dresses the white lines
with precision and formality.

She showcases the woodwork,
denier of dreams and maker of miracles,
and embraces the centre spot,
the site of all new beginnings.

While the
           clock
                    still   ticks
the scales can still tip
and anything is possible.

Imprints and echoes below
do nothing to slow her progress.
Expectation and anticipation
are borne of what went before.

After the frost, a softening thaw
and, in time, once more
we'll hear the thunderous,
wonderous, fan-fuelled roar.

To See It

She's a silver-shoed striker
a right foot crosser
a beezer of a smile
a 'go the extra mile'
a true team player
a braw pie eater
a cold weather warrior
with the ball a permanent extension of her foot.

So this evening her and I
will get our match-rags on
for a night in the girl's home stadium
the mighty Hampden.
Because they built it,
she will come.

Tonight we'll do each other's hair
hers in a Caroline Weir,
mine a classic Lisa Evans
as Erin tries to make history
in the manner of Jane Ross
scoring in four from four
in the hope we get three from three.

We'll be in our lucky seats
layered up, both feet in the camp.
Hungary for more
for World Cup-level more
because it's important that she sees it
because to see it, is to be it.

Let It Play

Twenty-three years,
and an hour before the 3pm bell
d'you think they'll roll out the telly
like the old days?

Classes full of weans
with Scotland tops snuck on
under school polo shirts
swapping Robertson, McGinn and Marshall
Panini stickers under the tables,

counting down the days,
then the hours, then the minutes
on the big clock in the classroom,

trying, and failing, to keep excited bums
on too-small plastic chairs,
to keep anticipation
from tipping over into hysteria.
Although hysteria is warranted:

'But are they gonna let us though?
I mean, who knows when the next time'll come
I could be 21, or 31, oh go on!'

And if not, 'can you call the school, Mum?
Have one of those "appointments"?
Doctors, dentists, I'll even get a haircut'.
I'll run home, Mum, put the shirt on
and be a part of history.
Me, a part of it.

Teachers are you with us now?
After all this year has thrown,
can you give us this?
I know you want to watch it too,

give us this time to celebrate,
or commiserate,
to let us feel the highs, and lows,
and pride at just being in the mix.
Let us be a part of it.

The maths test can wait
until tomorrow, no?
This?
This is our team,
This is our time,
Smart board, telly, iPad in the corner
Just let it play.

Odds On

Scanning the statistics
in the latest Twitter poll
France's chances are most favourable,
followed by Belgium, Spain –
no surprises there.

Scanning down,
down,
down,
a wee bit mair

there's Scotland 0.1% for the win
Hang on, 0.1%?
For the win?
so
you're telling me
there's a chance!?

The Whistle

The 'only for outdoors' ball thuds,
smacking off the freshly painted walls
a FIFA-induced din and despair
and a floor strewn with Match Attax collectibles.

The small boy laps the garden, arms aloft
executing his first Cruyff turn
round the washing pole,
dad teaches him Archie Gemmill's '78 for PE.

Strips pulled over jammies
navigating mops of hair,
socks, long forgotten,
get your daily dose of air.
The referee blew time
and the world paused,

on the sidelines nothing really stopped,
one man helps another up
the woman leaves her kids to sit
and does her bit.

Men and women venture out
donning masks and gloves in love
to get supplies and try to think
of the collective.

Rainbows appear everywhere
in chalk, in paint, in packages,
on doorsteps left with care
in place of hugs and being there.

The young girl lays out cones around the kitchen
and rolls up socks to play
the boy laughs on zoom at pictures
of his teammates as new babes

and the ball rolls on from home to home
across the globe. It sprinkles hope
as we find new ways to be together
while we hold our breath and wait.

Yes Kids, You Can Boogie

It's extra time, we've blown it
I'm sending the wee yin to bed:
she doesn't need the disappointment
this year's filled her head
with quite enough dread.

Somehow, we hang on
the thirty minutes done
as Griff walks up to the spot
the door creaks open,
the bairn appears,

a wee pyjama-clad beacon
a bed-ruffled mascot
drawn down the stairs
by magnitude and snacks
and potential jubilation.

One by one the hope, it grows
we are all David Marshall's glove
and Kenny McLean's foot
we are the
pause

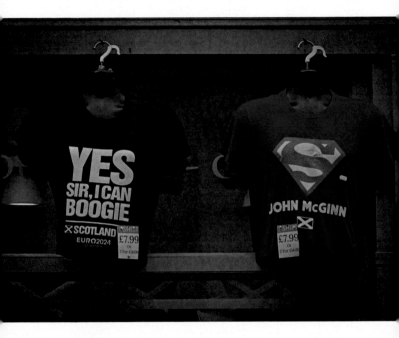

to wait for the thumbs up
then we are Scotland,
in the European championship.
We are couches used as trampolines
weans thrown in the air.

We are bedtimes long forgotten.
We are Ryan Christie's tears.
We are there.

Upon Our Shoulders
For Hampden Bowling Club, the home of world football

All tales deserve to be told,
but this one even more so than most.
As the roof sags under the weight of history
beaten down by the elements,
swollen by stories
raised up by the roar of the match days
should we just let it fall?

In this age of throw-away
and instant-one-click-replace-it-next-day
should we take a picture for Instagram
stick a filter on, and move on?

Or should we stretch out our arms
linked, ring-fenced protecting our piece of the story
extending a VIP cordon around our football square mile
a neon light that's clear to see from space:
this way to the first.

We know she needs our help
though she'd be too proud to ask for it,
standing stalwart and stooped
like a lighthouse guiding lost ships to shore
shining a spotlight on Scotland's place.

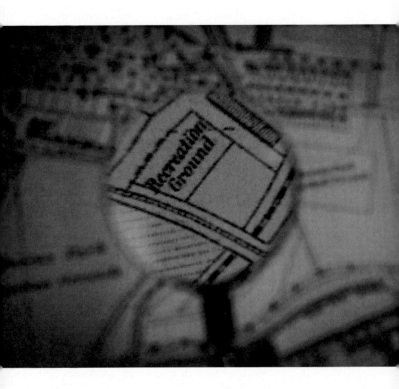

Picture the scene as we repair, restore and marvel
Japanese kintsugi-style
with a gold seam through the rotten beams.
She rises from the dust of Watson
and the Scotch Professors, to the dawn
of Marshall, Reilly, Robertson, Weir
and all those too wee now, but one day...

because once she's gone, she's gone.
So climb gently when you stand upon her shoulders
tread softly when you are raising up the game.
The years are a measure of her strength
not a reason to erase.

All firsts are worthy of remembering
but as you kick and pass and cheer
and weep away your Saturday
tread softly by *First Hampden*
pour gold into her seams, pass the magic on
and pay homage to this field of dreams.

We Are Scottish Football

We are in it for the big games
We are saving our lucky seats
We're securing the season tickets,
the transfers
We are new strips revealed

We are the buzz of club signings
We are 'It's going to be our year'
We are staying off the bottom
We are summer games
and mid-week nights under the lights
We are VAR – aye, right!

We are derbies, away days
fixtures in the back of beyond.
The road trips, the packed bus
the snacks
the tunes

We are 'Could we just nick it,
if we get an early goal?'
We are the upsets
the underdogs
We are that beautiful overhead kick

We are 'That was rubbish
but same time next week, yeah?'
We are avoiding play-offs
pitches – pristine and waiting
We are that glistening net
the shine off the brand new ball

We are new managers
breaking in the new boots
We are looking over our shoulders
checking the six o'clock
to get to the top six
We are the pies!

We are phone-ins
opinions
panels
What's your point caller?
We are the armchair experts
the bar-propping scotch professors

We are the unbeaten run
the clean sheet
We have Europe in our grasp

We are full crowds
packed out
We are 'Refereeeeee!'
'Offside, surely!'
We are going to do it this year

We are the new songs
the big drums
the frost-bitten toes
the squeaky bums

We are extra time
just in time
down the line
he's off his line
out of time!

We are the highs and lows and anything goes.
We are Scottish Football

One More

Go on!
Just one more, for us
for the zoom-fatigued,
the weary
the ever hopeful, us.

Just one more
perfect breakaway
one more well-timed cross
one more chance to celebrate
John's acrobatics in the box.

Just one more heave towards the dream
let's swing our housecoats round our heads
one more perfect strike,
we'll jump up and down on unmade beds.

Go on give us that, and all of that
then give us something more.
Because although we're not in Hampden
we're all Scotland after all.

Glasgow, *My First Love*

Autumn has settled
on Glasgow's sandstone.
The sky is a brilliant blue
clouds in soft vapour trails
tickling the tips of chimneys
and flagpoles.

Underfoot the pavements
slip, washed to a shine
with early morning rain
as men in Glengarry hats
and half-kilts stumble
their way out the dark.

My city is gleaming: first
lights of Christmas wink
from every bar, auburn
crisp of hedgerows
warm, and that sky:

cobalt and pure white,
I am in love.

Away Days
For Cammy and Jack

I know I've given you a rucksack, Jack,
would've been easier to be Blue or Green
but there's something special
in supporting your home team.

There's history here,
of games lost and won
memories crafted through the years
and new ones with you, son.

The truth is I wouldn't change it:
the car journeys, and the chats,
the crack-of-dawn alarms and drive-thrus
the rush to get you there and back.

The permanent away days.
You: too big to be my baby
but still wee enough to stand on the seats
my arm around you – steady.

You turned your face to mine
the other day after a crushing defeat
and said you love these days we have
and that's enough for me.

Acknowledgements

MY THANKS TO the Hampden Collection volunteers for their tireless work creating Football's Square Mile and providing space for football, history and poetry to meet and grow together.

'Football's Square Mile' is a free, open-air museum in Glasgow and each site tells the (rarely told) story of how Scotland invented, then exported, the modern passing game of football to the world. Many of the poems in this collection are inspired by each of the 21 sites of historical significance. https://www.footballssquaremile.com

Some of these poems have appeared online through the Hampden Collection, in *Nutmeg Magazine* and *Football Is Poetry* (2).

'The Dale' was commissioned by Clydesdale Cricket Club to mark their 175th birthday in 2023 and 'We Are Scottish Football' was recorded as a film poem for BBC Scotland to mark the start of the 2022/23 Scottish Premiership season. 'That Guy', 'Zero Sum Game' and 'Level Playing Field' were commissioned poems as part of a football and hate crime project.

Luath Press Limited

committed to publishing well written books worth reading

LUATH PRESS takes its name from Robert Burns, whose little collie Luath (*Gael.*, swift or nimble) tripped up Jean Armour at a wedding and gave him the chance to speak to the woman who was to be his wife and the abiding love of his life. Burns called one of the 'Twa Dogs' Luath after Cuchullin's hunting dog in Ossian's *Fingal*. Luath Press was established in 1981 in the heart of Burns country, and is now based a few steps up the road from Burns' first lodgings on Edinburgh's Royal Mile. Luath offers you distinctive writing with a hint of unexpected pleasures.

Most bookshops in the UK, the US, Canada, Australia, New Zealand and parts of Europe, either carry our books in stock or can order them for you. To order direct from us, please send a £sterling cheque, postal order, international money order or your credit card details (number, address of cardholder and expiry date) to us at the address below. Please add post and packing as follows: UK – £1.00 per delivery address; overseas surface mail – £2.50 per delivery address; overseas airmail – £3.50 for the first book to each delivery address, plus £1.00 for each additional book by airmail to the same address. If your order is a gift, we will happily enclose your card or message at no extra charge.

Luath Press Limited

543/2 Castlehill
The Royal Mile
Edinburgh EH1 2ND
Scotland
Telephone: 0131 225 4326 (24 hours)
Email: sales@luath.co.uk
Website: www.luath.co.uk